EXPLAINING THE STAMP AND TOWNSHEND ACTS

US History for Kids
Children's American History

In this book, we are going to cover the Stamp and Townshend Acts, an important part of United States History before the colonies were independent from Britain. So let's get right to it!

WHAT EVENTS LED UP TO THE STAMP ACT?

Even though the American colonies were under British rule, they had been ruling themselves for over 150 years. Then, Britain decided to start enforcing laws that would prevent the colonists from moving westward. In addition to that, they started to tax them.

American Colonies

1745
Semper Eadem Three farthings
All of a Stamp
Family Vault lie
ou'd never to rise
Remaine of
arthmen   ship
wise B
&c.
CONWAY
ROCKINGHAM
GRAFTON
Manchester
Halifax
Leeds
Burial serv
Funeral Sermon by Anti Sejanus
Burial of the Dog
The American Ship 1765

SEARCH WARRANTS ON SHIPS

Ship inspectors had long had the duty to search ships that were going to the colonies. However, they hadn't actively started to use these general search warrants until around 1765. Now violators were prosecuted and they didn't even get a trial by jury!

THE STAMP ACT OF 1765

All of these changes were brought on by the Seven Years' War that Britain had with other European countries, including France. That war had been very costly and now Britain was levying taxes to make up for that cost.

Bostonians reading the Stamp Act

by Mr. Thos. Major Engraved Two Copper Plates for the One Penny Duty on News Papers &c. ... ber'd from 151 to 175 the other from 176 to 200 Inclusive & the Impressions whereof are here on this ... In Witness whereof We have hereunto set our Hands the 10 May 1765   By Order of the Commiss...

hereby Acknowledge to have this Day Received back the Above mentiond Copper Plates & ... ... other Plates & Dies used in ... ... according to the ... ... Witness our Hands ...

Proof sheet of 1 penny stamps

Every single piece of paper was taxed. Legal documents, newspapers, and even playing cards were taxed! There was an official stamp to indicate that these documents had been paid for and this is where the name "Stamp Act" came from.

The colonists were outraged by these taxes. The British government didn't see the problem. After all, the taxes the American colonists were being asked to pay were much lower than those of the citizens in Britain.

Also, the money raised from these taxes was used in part to defend the colonies and only paid for about one-third of the overall cost of keeping British troops there.

British Troops

THE COLONISTS' VIEW OF THE STAMP ACT

The colonists didn't understand why the British wanted to keep soldiers in North America. Now that the threat from other European countries was gone, it didn't make sense that the colonists should have to pay for keeping British troops around.

It was true, that citizens in England paid much more in taxes, but the colonists had their lives at stake. At this point in time, it wasn't easy living in North America. They had to fight Native Americans, clear land, and many citizens died building colonies to give glory to the British Empire. These taxes seemed very insulting to them. They didn't want to pay them!

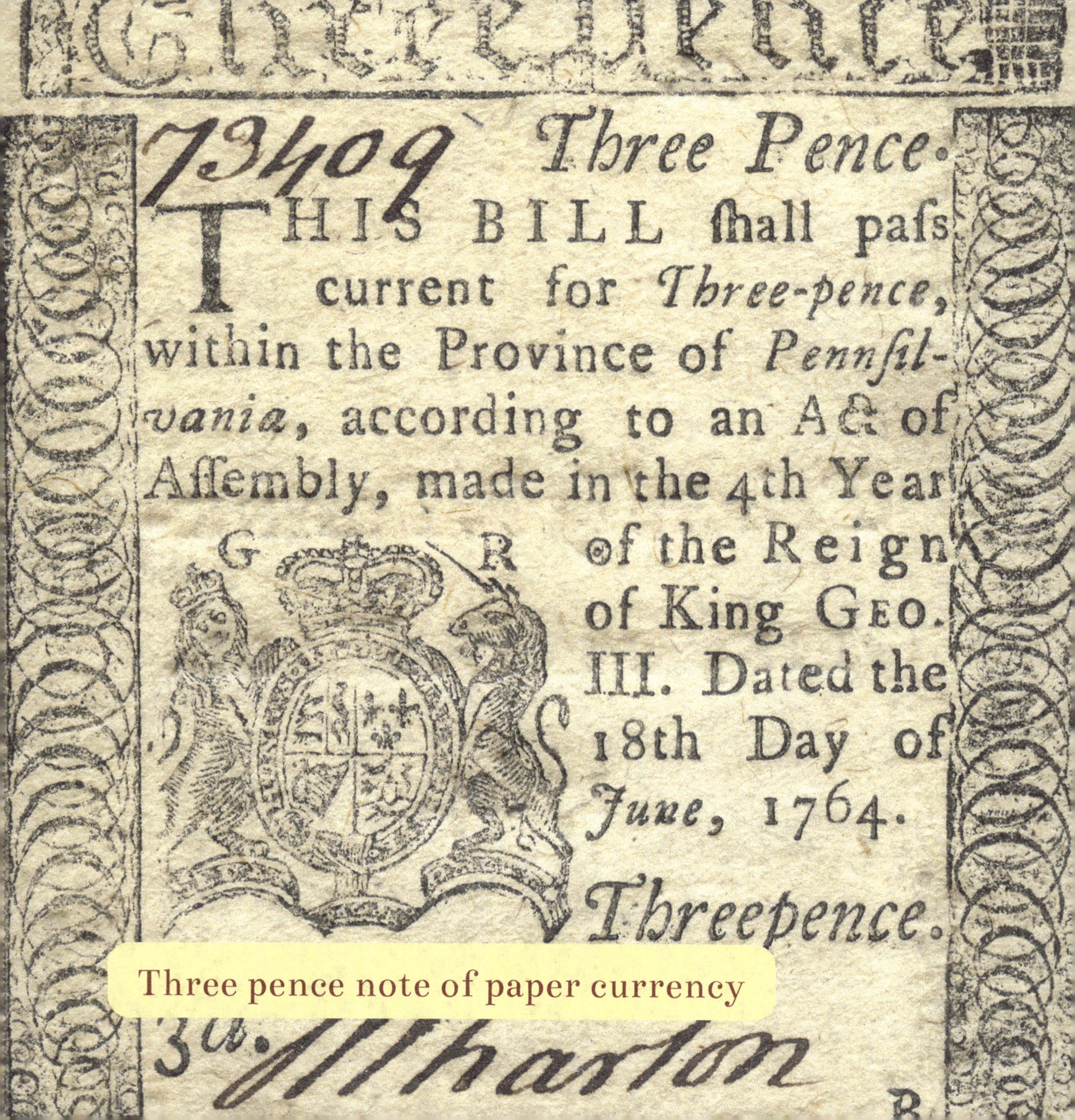

Three pence note of paper currency

THE SUGAR ACT AND CURRENCY ACT

This tax wasn't the first attempt to tax the colonies. The British parliament had passed the Sugar Act and Currency Act in 1764. These taxes were collected at ports so there was some potential for the colonists to circumvent them.

These taxes were more indirect, so the everyday consumer didn't notice them so much. But a tax on every single sheet of paper and document! This was outrageous! The colonists began to appeal to the British government for relief from the Stamp Act tax. Unlike other British subjects, the colonists didn't have any representation in the British parliament. The idea of "no taxation without representation" was born.

Stamp Act riots

Seven Years War

THE FRENCH AND INDIAN WAR

During the Seven Years' War, there was a companion war being fought closer to home in the Americas. From 1754 to 1763, the British had helped their colonies win a war against the French and the Native Americans.

This war was called the French and Indian War. Eventually, the colonies won, but they had the help of British troops. This was another reason why the British government felt that the colonies should be taxed. After all, this war was fought on North American soil.

French Indian War

Battle of Plassey

In addition to not having representation in Parliament, the representatives in the colonies had no say in the amount of the tax or how the tax should be levied. This lack of control sparked unrest in the colonies.

HOW DID THE COLONIES REACT?

The colonies began a violent protest. They refused to pay the Stamp Act taxes. The collectors of the taxes were threatened and forced to quit their jobs. Citizens burned the stamped paper in the streets. They went so far as to boycott British products and merchants, which simply means they wouldn't buy their products or go into their stores.

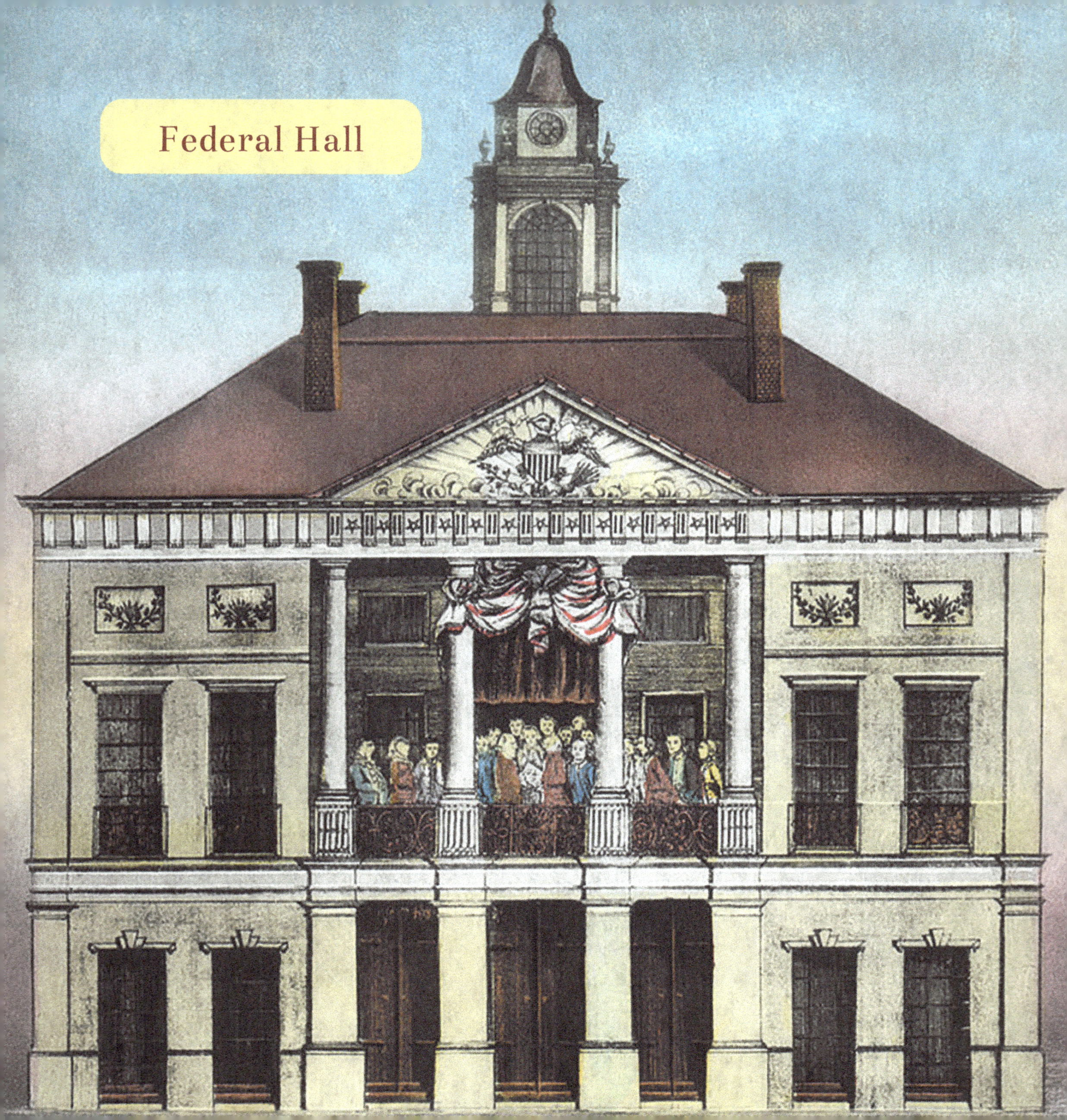
Federal Hall

In fact, they felt so strongly against the taxes that they called a meeting where representatives of all the colonies got together. This meeting was called the Stamp Act Congress. In 1765, they convened in New York City from October 7-25. They organized and prepared a unified written protest of the Act to present to the British government.

WHO WERE THE SONS OF LIBERTY?

At this time, groups of American patriots were formed. They called themselves the Sons of Liberty. Eventually, they would become an influential group during the American Revolution. Their protests of the taxes started to hurt the sales of British goods. After all these protests, the British did away with the Stamp Act on March 18, 1766. However, they still wanted to keep the colonies in line. The same day that the Stamp Act was stopped, they issued a Declaratory Act. This Act stated that the parliament in Britain had the right to collect taxes and pass laws for the colonies, whether they had representation or not.

Boston Tea Party

MORE AND MORE TAXES

Even after this protest, the British government continued to tax the colonies. They added a tax to tea that would eventually lead to the Boston Tea Party, an event where colonists protested the tax by throwing tea overboard. All this unrest between Britain and its colonies in North America eventually led to the American Revolution.

SOME INTERESTING FACTS ABOUT THE STAMP ACT

Colonists had to use British money to pay for the tax since colonial money couldn't be used.

JOHN ADAMS

Future president of the United States, John Adams was involved in writing a series of documents that protested the tax. He also started the Sons of Liberty.

The British government thought the tax was completely fair. They really didn't think they were oppressing the colonies.

CHARLES TOWNSHEND

THE TOWNSHEND ACTS

In 1767, the British government levied new taxes specifically on imports of paper, glass, tea, lead, and paint. Charles Townshend introduced this law into parliament so this is where the law got its name.

The Townshend Acts also took away some of the freedoms the colonists were used to. In Boston, the British set up a special customs board designed to collect the taxes. They also set up courts to bring justice to any smugglers who tried to get away with not paying the taxes. There were no local juries in these courts, so the British had full authority to go into houses and businesses to search for stolen goods and prosecute offenders.

2
3
4

WHY DID THE BRITISH INACT THE TOWNSHEND ACTS?

The British were tired of funding the colonies and wanted to collect money so that the colonies would pay for themselves. These taxes were used to pay the salaries of government officials, such as judges and governors. Once again, just as they did with the Stamp Act, the colonists protested.

The more that the British taxed them, the more the colonists protested. The colonists were used to their independence. The Stamp Act and the Townshend Acts continued to spark a revolutionary attitude in the colonists. They were beginning to think about forming their own government and getting out from under the thumb of British rule. This was the beginning of the seeds of revolution.

American Revolution

British Parliament

WHY WERE THE COLONISTS SO UPSET?

Perhaps if they had representatives in the British parliament, the colonists wouldn't have protested so violently. They just didn't want to be taxed if they had no right to how they were governed. They felt that it was unconstitutional. The cost of the tax was less important to them than the principle that they shouldn't be taxed without representation. The taxes continued to cause more and more unrest.

John Dickinson, who would later author the Articles of Confederation, authored a group of essays called Letters from a Farmer in Pennsylvania. These documents stated that paying the taxes would only lead the British to tax the colonists more.

JOHN DICKINSON

Merchants living in the colonies banded together to organize boycotts of all British-made goods. They also smuggled in goods to prevent paying the taxes. This was a dangerous activity and many were caught and prosecuted.

Protests in Boston turned very violent when British soldiers killed colonists in the streets. This event became known as the Boston Massacre.

Boston Massacre
BUTCHER'S HALL
CUSTOM HOUSE

JOHN HANCOCK

SOME INTERESTING FACTS ABOUT THE TOWNSHEND ACTS

» The British stopped most of the taxation in 1770 except for the tea tax. That tax was continued when they passed the Tea Act in 1773.

» Charles Townshend died in September 1767, so he never saw the devastation the law he had proposed caused.

» The American colonists didn't want to pay taxes to a government that didn't think of them as citizens with full rights. They wanted to be represented in parliament.

» John Hancock, later one of the signers of the Declaration of Independence and a Founding Father of the United States, was once accused of smuggling. Custom agents from Britain searched his ship.

Now you know more about the Stamp Act and Townshend Acts and how they led up to the Revolutionary War. You can find more History books from Baby Professor by searching the website of your favorite book retailer.

Visit
BABY PROFESSOR
EDUCATION KIDS
www.BabyProfessorBooks.com
to download Free Baby Professor eBooks
and view our catalog of new and exciting
Children's Books

9 798886 943255 1